MADE IN THE
U.S.A.

SNOWBOARDS

From Start to Finish

Tanya Lee Stone

Photographs by Gale Zucker

BLACKBIRCH PRESS, INC.
WOODBRIDGE, CONNECTICUT

For Laurie "Suss" Suzanne   —TLS

Special Thanks

The author and the publisher would like to thank Scott Rivers, Jennifer Sweeney, Tim Brodhagen, and Amy Barrett for their generous help in putting this project together.

Published by Blackbirch Press, Inc.
260 Amity Road
Woodbridge, CT 06525

e-mail: staff@blackbirch.com
Web site: www.blackbirch.com

©2000 by Blackbirch Press, Inc.
First Edition

Printed in Singapore

10 9 8 7 6 5 4 3 2 1

Photo Credits: All photographs © Gale Zucker except pages 2 & 3 (©Burton Snowboards 2000 courtesy Burton snowboards); page 14 (©Mark Gallup, courtesy Burton Snowboards); page 15 (© Fosbrook Photography, Courtesy Burton Snowboards); page 23 (© 2000 Backhill Snowboarding Co.); page 31 (© Fosbrook Photography, Courtesy Burton Snowboards).

Library of Congress Cataloging-in-Publication Data

Stone, Tanya Lee.
Snowboards: from start to finish / Tanya Lee Stone ; photographs by Gale Zucker.
    p.   cm.   (Made in the U.S.A.)
    Includes bibliographical references and index.
    Summary: Describes how snowboards are manufactured and provides a history of the sport of snowboarding.
    ISBN 1-56711-480-6 (hard : alk. paper)
    1. Snowboards—Design and construction—juvenile literature.
[1. Snowboards. 2. Snowboarding.] I. Zucker, Gale, ill. II. Title. III. Series.
GV857.S57 S84   2000
796.9—dc21   00-009059

Contents

Snowboard Leaders	4
Starting at the Bottom	6
The Core of the Board	8
Tips, Tails and Sidewalls	10
More Tips and Tails	12
Building the Board	16
Board Baking	20
No Bumps or Bubbles	22
Trimming and Shaping	24
Grinding and Buffing	26
Slicked and Screened	28
Almost Perfect	29
Johnny Robot on the Job	30
Glossary	32
For More Information	32
Index	32

Have you ever heard of a half-pipe, a McTwist, or a pow turn? If you are one of the 6 million snowboarders in the world, you know those words describe snowboarding moves. Snowboarding is one of the fastest growing sports on the planet. It even became an Olympic event in 1998.

Snowboarders need great boards to ride. This is the story of how snow-boards are made.

Thirteen-year-old Mike Rencz soars through the air on his snowboard.

3

Snowboard Leaders

Burton Snowboards, in
Burlington, Vermont, is the
world's largest snowboard
brand. Their products are sold
in 30 countries.

❄

*Burton's main office and retail
store is just a few miles away
from the factory.*

There are many different models of snowboards, each one designed to fit a certain-sized body and a certain kind of rider. Most days, the factory produces three different models. No matter what the model, style, or design, every snowboard starts out the same way: as a piece of wood.

A rider tries on boots and a board to see how they fit.

Starting at the Bottom

The only snowboard part that is not made at the factory is the picture that goes on the bottom. These graphics come to the factory in rectangular sheets of plastic. Before they can be cut, a computer programs the specific length and width of a board and creates a template. A template is the master set-up, with measurements and specifications that are used for every board of that type. Each board has its own template.

Above: A pile of graphics sheets are ready to be cut.
Right, top and bottom: The sheets are lined up on a template and cut.

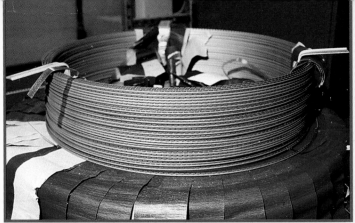

Other materials are also prepared at this stage. Metal that will go around the edges of a board is cut from large spools. It is bent to fit each model type. Gummy tape is also stretched out and prepared for various models.

A worker programs the planing machine computer.

The Core of the Board

The wooden layer, or core, of a snowboard is cut from both hard and soft woods. The wood is pressed together in a special way to make it strong. Then a machine cuts binding holes in the core. The bindings attach a snowboard boot to a board.

A computer is then used to program the right length and width of the model being cut. The planing machine trims the rectangular core into a rounded board shape. After it is planed, the core now has a tip (front), a tail (back), and sides. Finally, a milling machine trims the core boards to make them the correct thickness.

The planing machine holds and cuts three boards at a time.

Tips, Tails and Sidewalls

The next step is to prepare the front, back, and edges of a board. A flexible plastic material that won't crack in the cold is used. This material protects against moisture and helps to hold the board together. Workers staple the plastic tips, tails, and sidewalls to the front, back, and edges of the board core.

A variety of flexible plastic tips, tails, and sidewalls are attached to the core.

❄

Sidewalls and tails are stapled into place.

More Tips and Tails

At this stage, the board core still needs more work. Staples are hammered to prevent them from sticking up. Any overlap of plastic between the sidewalls and the tip and tail is snipped away. Then a thin fiberglass mesh sheet is hammered into the binding holes. The inserts that will attach the bindings to the board are also put in place. The mesh keeps the inserts from spinning. The boards are now ready for the next stage of assembly, called layup.

A worker cuts overlapping plastic between a sidewall and a tip.

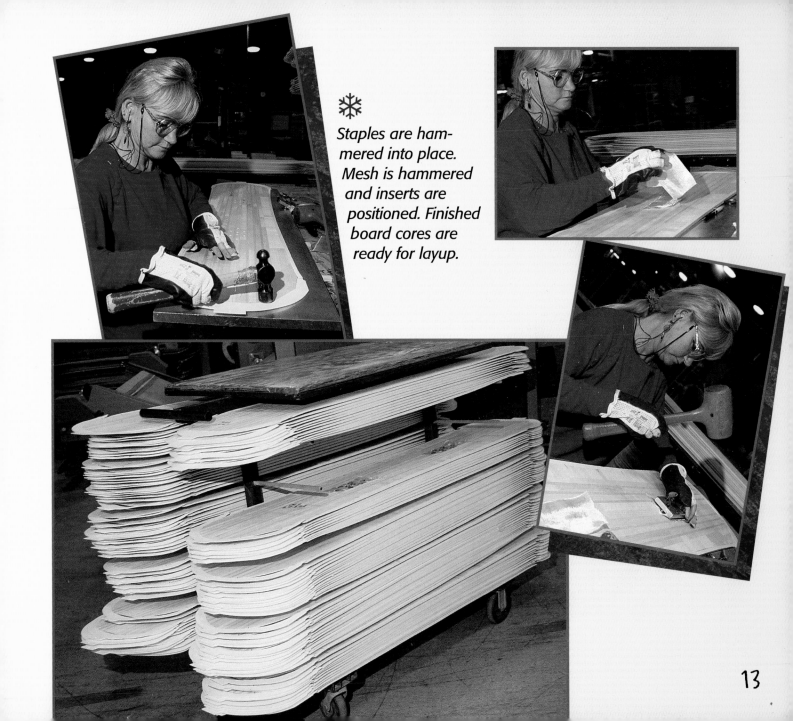

❄

Staples are hammered into place. Mesh is hammered and inserts are positioned. Finished board cores are ready for layup.

13

The Sport That Jake Built

Many people feel that Jake Burton Carpenter invented snowboarding. But there was a toy that came before the snowboard. It was called the

Snurfer. Jake played with it in the mid-1960s and loved "surfing" on snow. Ten years went by, but little other "snow surfing" equipment was made. He left his job in 1977 and built the world's first snowboard factory. He and his friends used every room of a Vermont farmhouse to make, sell, and fix the earliest Burton boards. At that time, only skiers were allowed to use ski lifts at the busiest mountain resorts. Anyone who wanted to snowboard had to hike up the mountain. Jake knew that unless ski lifts were opened to snowboarders, the sport would never have a chance.

Jake Burton Carpenter

Some of the first Burton snowboards.

Within a few years, he convinced most Vermont resorts to open their lifts. Eventually, many resorts across the country followed. This made the sport grow quickly. The need for faster and better boards grew quickly, too. Jake Burton Carpenter saw that need and filled it. Today, Burton snowboards is the largest snowboard brand in the world.

Above: The metal plate is air-brushed.
Right: The graphic is put down.

Building the Board

In layup, all the parts are put together in a mold. First, the bottom of the metal mold is put down and air-brushed clean. The bottom graphic goes down next. Metal edges are put on, clamped in place, and spacers are attached to allow room for glue.

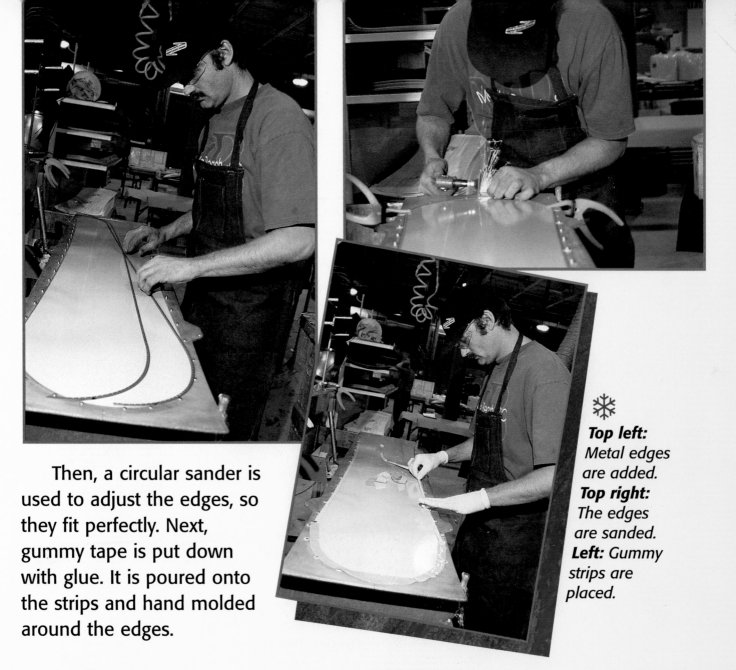

Then, a circular sander is used to adjust the edges, so they fit perfectly. Next, gummy tape is put down with glue. It is poured onto the strips and hand molded around the edges.

❄

Top left: Metal edges are added.
Top right: The edges are sanded.
Left: Gummy strips are placed.

A sheet of fiberglass goes down next, and more glue is applied by hand. Then, the wood core is placed. More gummy strips are put around the sidewalls, tip, and tail. A second sheet of fiberglass is added, along with more glue. Finally, the top graphic sheet is placed. The whole piece is air-brushed clean, and the top of the metal mold is secured on top.

Top left: *The first fiberglass sheet is placed.*
Bottom left: *The wood core is put down.*
Above: *The second fiberglass sheet is placed.*

Left and top: The graphic goes down and is air-brushed.
Above: A finished mold is carried to the press.

19

Left: *A board is placed in a press.*
Below: *Presses bake boards for 10 minutes at a high temperature.*

Board Baking

Once layup is complete, a board is put in a press and baked for 10 minutes at 190° Fahrenheit. This hardens the glue and sets the pieces permanently. After it is baked, the board is taken out of the mold and the excess glue is scraped off. The board is then given to an inspector.

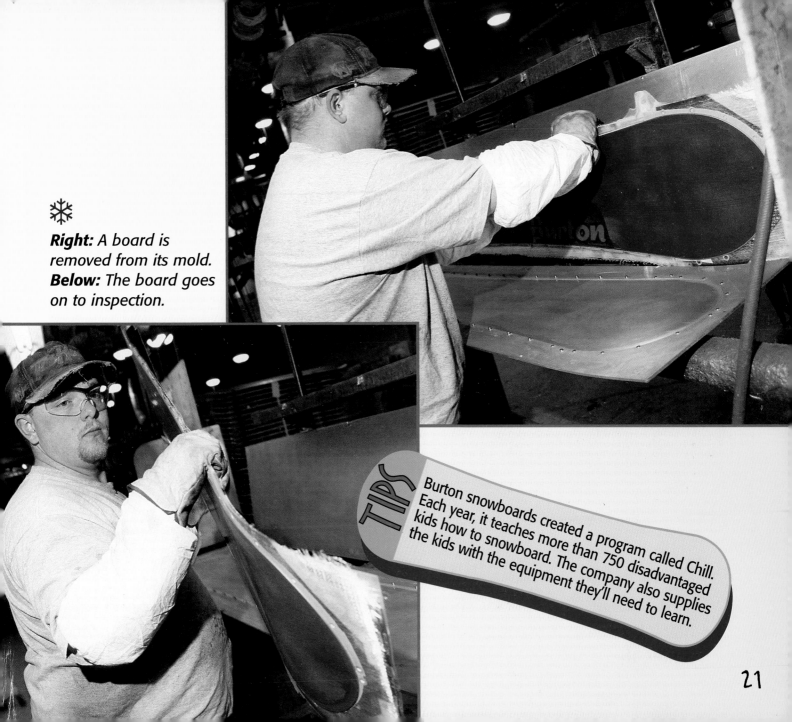

❄

Right: *A board is removed from its mold.*
Below: *The board goes on to inspection.*

TIPS

Burton snowboards created a program called Chill. Each year, it teaches more than 750 disadvantaged kids how to snowboard. The company also supplies the kids with the equipment they'll need to learn.

21

Top, left and middle: *An inspector uses his eyes and hands to check for any defects in a board.*
Below: *A board is passed into the trimming room.*

No Bumps or Bubbles

At this stage, an inspector checks the board to make sure there are no stray hairs, bubbles, or bumps. If it passes inspection, the board is passed through a hole that goes into a room where the edges are trimmed and shaped.

Snowboard Stylin'

Kids are a major force in snowboarding. The U.S. Open Snowboarding Championships now has a Junior Jam section for kids ages 5 to 14. Thirteen-year-olds Shaun White and Mike Rencz have led the way in this event, showing that young snowboarders can hold their own on the mountains. And girls are no exception. Shaun's sister, Kari White, is a top rider in her age group. These young, fearless riders help to push the sport to new limits every day.

Fifteen-year-old Kari White

23

Trimming and Shaping

Workers wear eye, ear, and mouth protection in the trim-and-shape room. A band saw is used to trim the excess material off the board's edges. A large circular sander is used to shape the sidewalls, tip, and tail.
The board is passed back through a hole when it is finished.

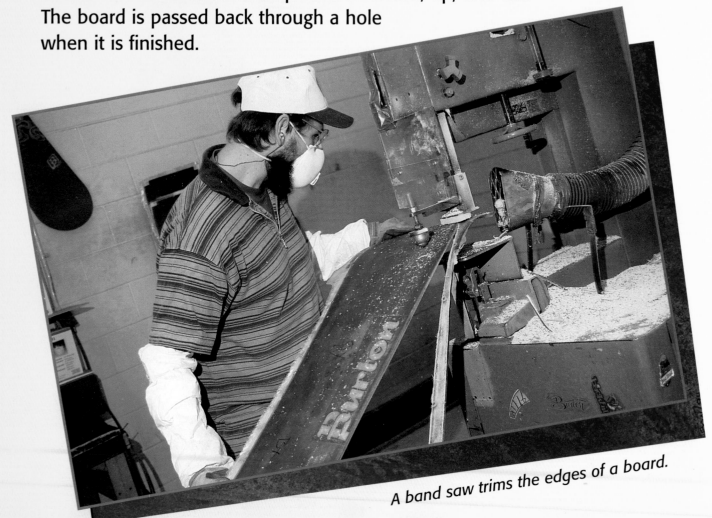

A band saw trims the edges of a board.

Above: *A tip is shaped on a large, circular sander.*
Right: *Sidewalls are shaped on the sander.*

25

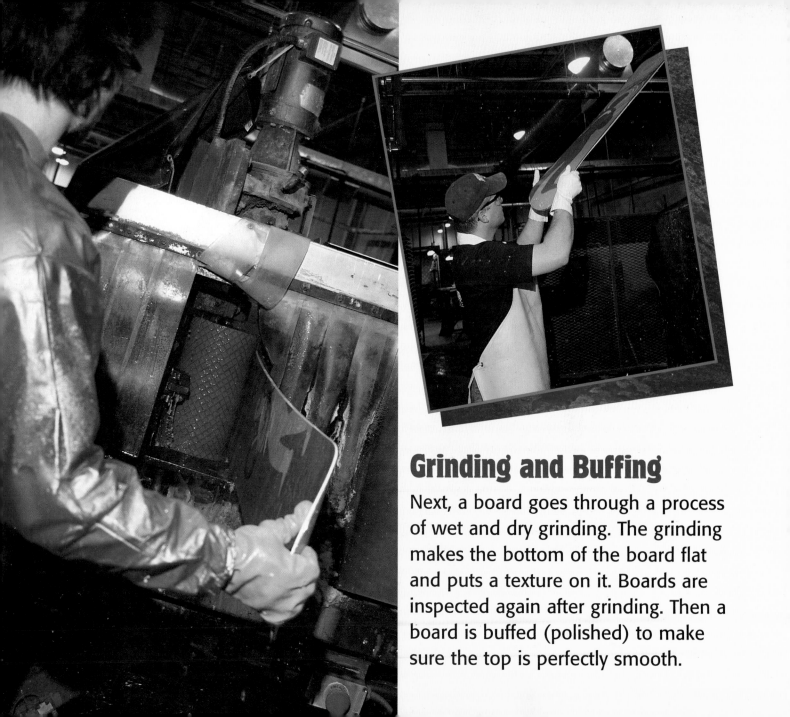

Grinding and Buffing

Next, a board goes through a process of wet and dry grinding. The grinding makes the bottom of the board flat and puts a texture on it. Boards are inspected again after grinding. Then a board is buffed (polished) to make sure the top is perfectly smooth.

Opposite left: *A board is put through a wet grinder.*
Opposite right: *A worker inspects a board after grinding.*
Above: *A board is buffed.*

Left: An image on a silk screen is placed on top of a board.
Bottom left: A worker spreads the paint through the screen to form an image on the board.
Below: The loop and the hatch marks were screened onto this board.

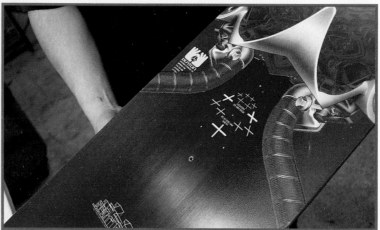

Slicked and Screened

Now a board is ready to be lacquered. This gives it a slick, glossy coating. The board goes through a series of ovens that apply lacquer and let it harden. This takes about 20 minutes. Once a board is cooled, the final images are silk-screened on. These are small graphics such as a name, logo, or number.

Almost Perfect

Next, a final buffing and inspection is done. Then, a drill is used to trim the excess material out of the insert holes to clean them up.

Top right: *A board is buffed and inspected.*
Right and below: *Workers use drills to trim material out of insert holes.*

29

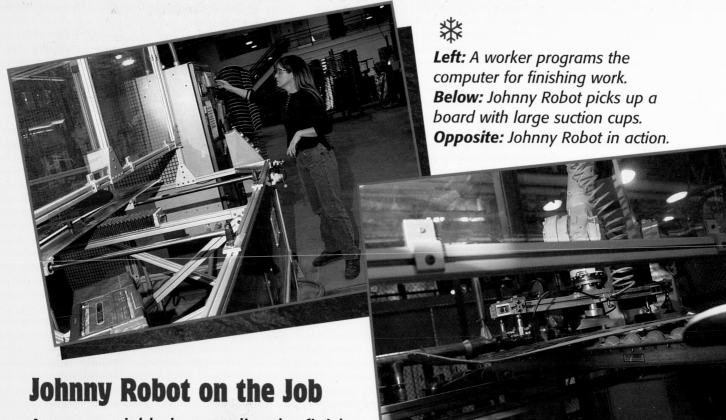

Johnny Robot on the Job

A very special helper applies the finishing touches. A machine called Johnny Robot, perfectly shapes each board.

A computer is programmed with the specific shape of a board model and all the angles of the edges, tip, and tail. One station does the edges and another does the tip and tail. Once Johnny Robot is finished, a worker polishes the board again and packs it in plastic. Now it is ready to zoom down slippery slopes anywhere in the world!

Glossary

Binding the fastening that holds a boot to a snowboard or ski.

Fiberglass a flexible material made of fine threads of glass that is durable and will not catch fire.

Layup the process of assembling the different parts of a snowboard.

Prototype an original model from which something is made.

Sidewalls the side edges of a snowboard.

Tail the back edge of a snowboard.

Tip the front edge of a snowboard.

For More Information

Books

Christopher, Matt. *Snowboard Maverick*. Boston, MA: Little, Brown & Company, 1997.

Guthrie, Robert. *Hotdogging and Snowboarding* (Action Sports Series). Minneapolis, MN: Capstone Press, 1992.

Jensen, Julie. *Beginning Snowboarding* (Beginning Sports Series). Minneapolis, MN: Lerner Publications, 1995.

McKenna, A.T. *Big-Air Snowboarding* (Extreme Sports Series). Minneapolis, MN: Capstone Press, 1999.

Web Site

Burton Snowboards
Learn about the history of snowboarding and the history of Burton Snowboards, read short profiles of Jake Burton and other famous riders, find out where you can learn to ride, and take a mini-tour of the factory—**www.burton.com**

Index

Buff, 26, 27, 29
Burlington, VT, 4
Burton Snowboards, 4, 21
Carpenter, Jake Burton, 14–15
Computer, 6, 9, 30
Core 8, 9–10 12, 13, 18

Graphics, 6, 16, 18, 19, 28
Grinding, 26–27
Gummy tape, 7, 17, 18
Inspector, 20, 22
Johnny Robot, 30
Layup, 12, 16
Metal, 7, 16, 17, 18

Milling machine, 9
Olympic, 3
Planing machine, 9
Plastic, 10, 12
Press, 20
Rencz, Mike, 3, 23
Sander, 24, 25
Silk-screened, 28

Snowboarders, 3, 23
Snurfer, 13
U.S. Open Snowboarding Championships, 23
White, Kari, 23
White, Shaun, 23
Wood, 5, 8